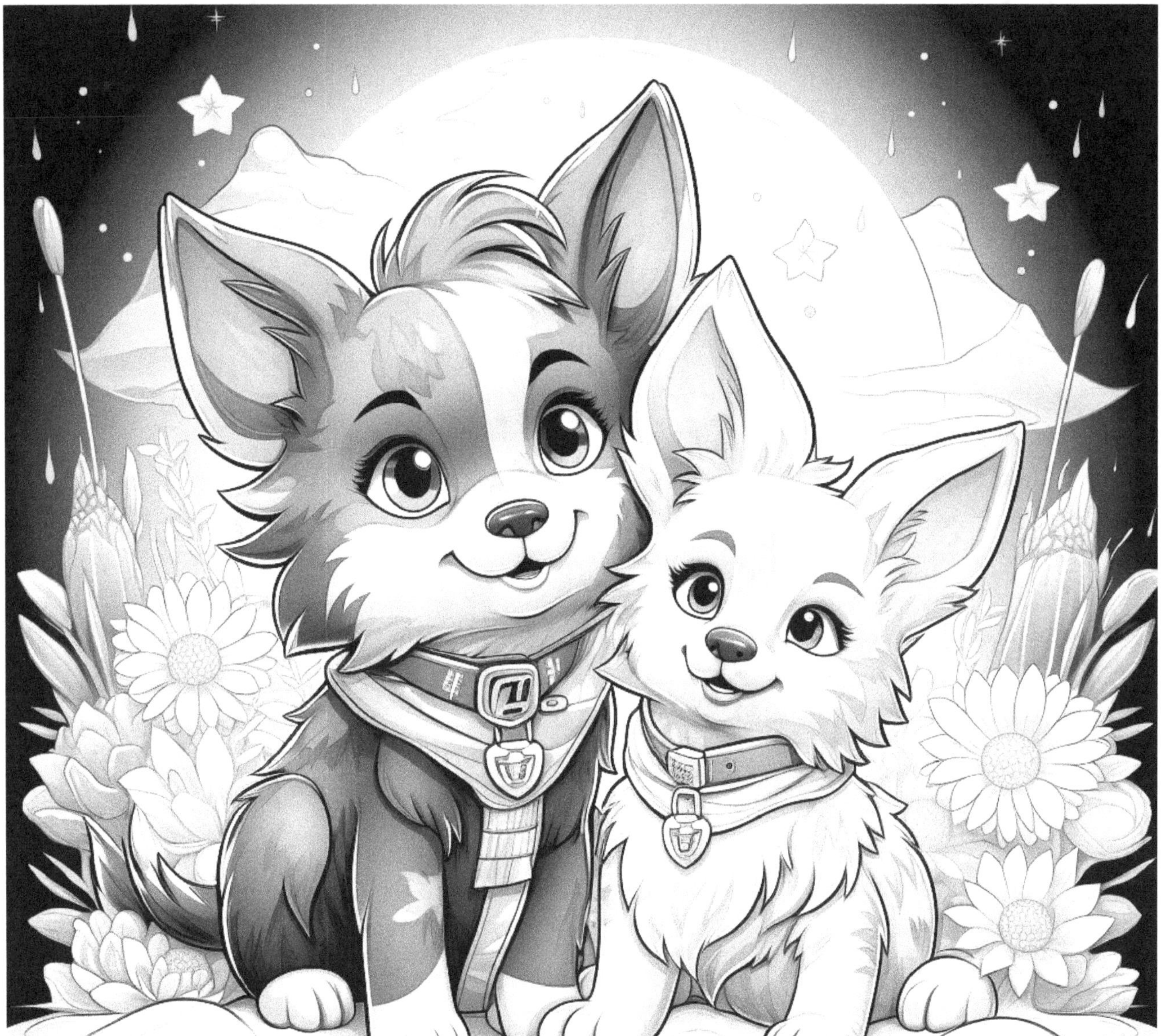

THIS COLORING BOOK
BELONGS TO:

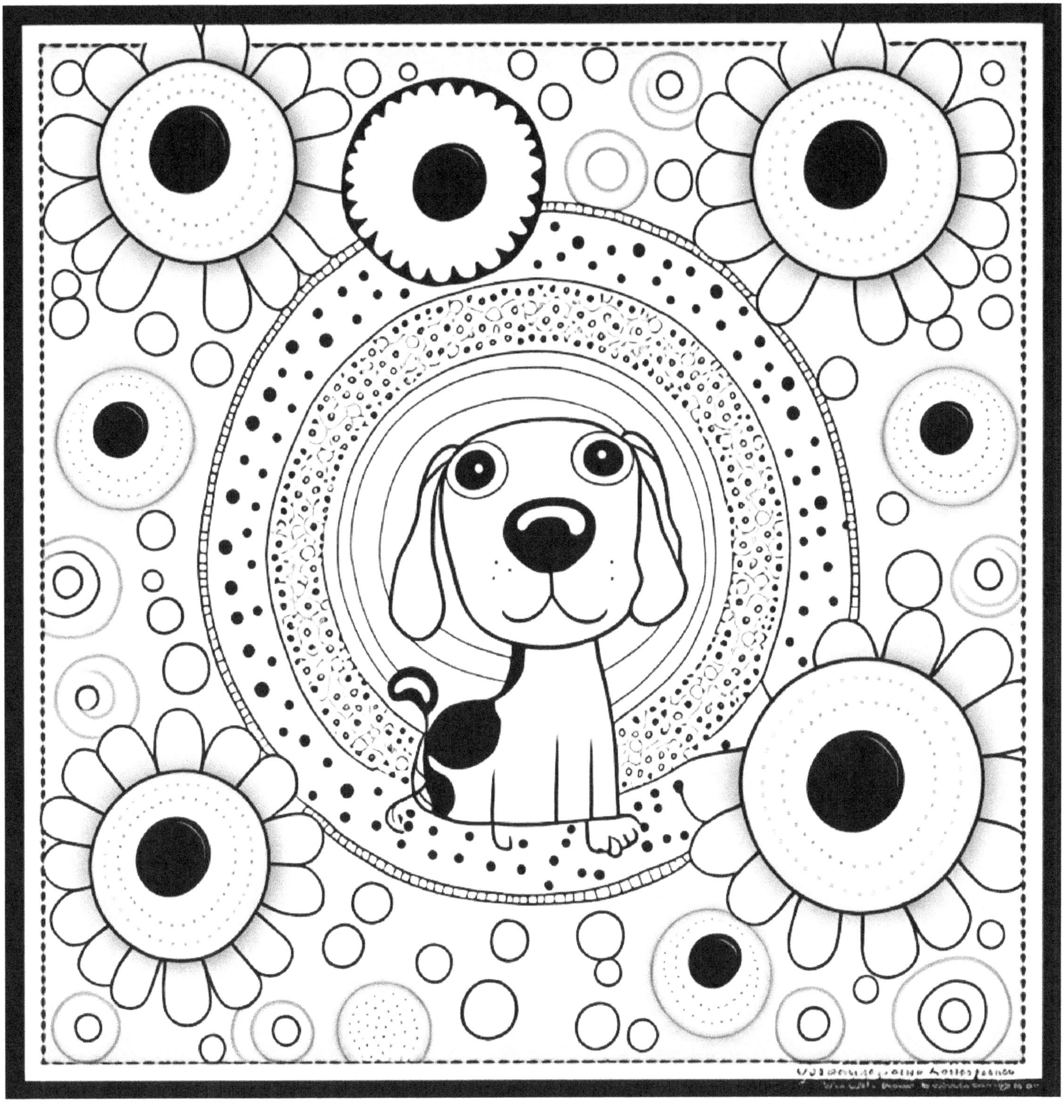

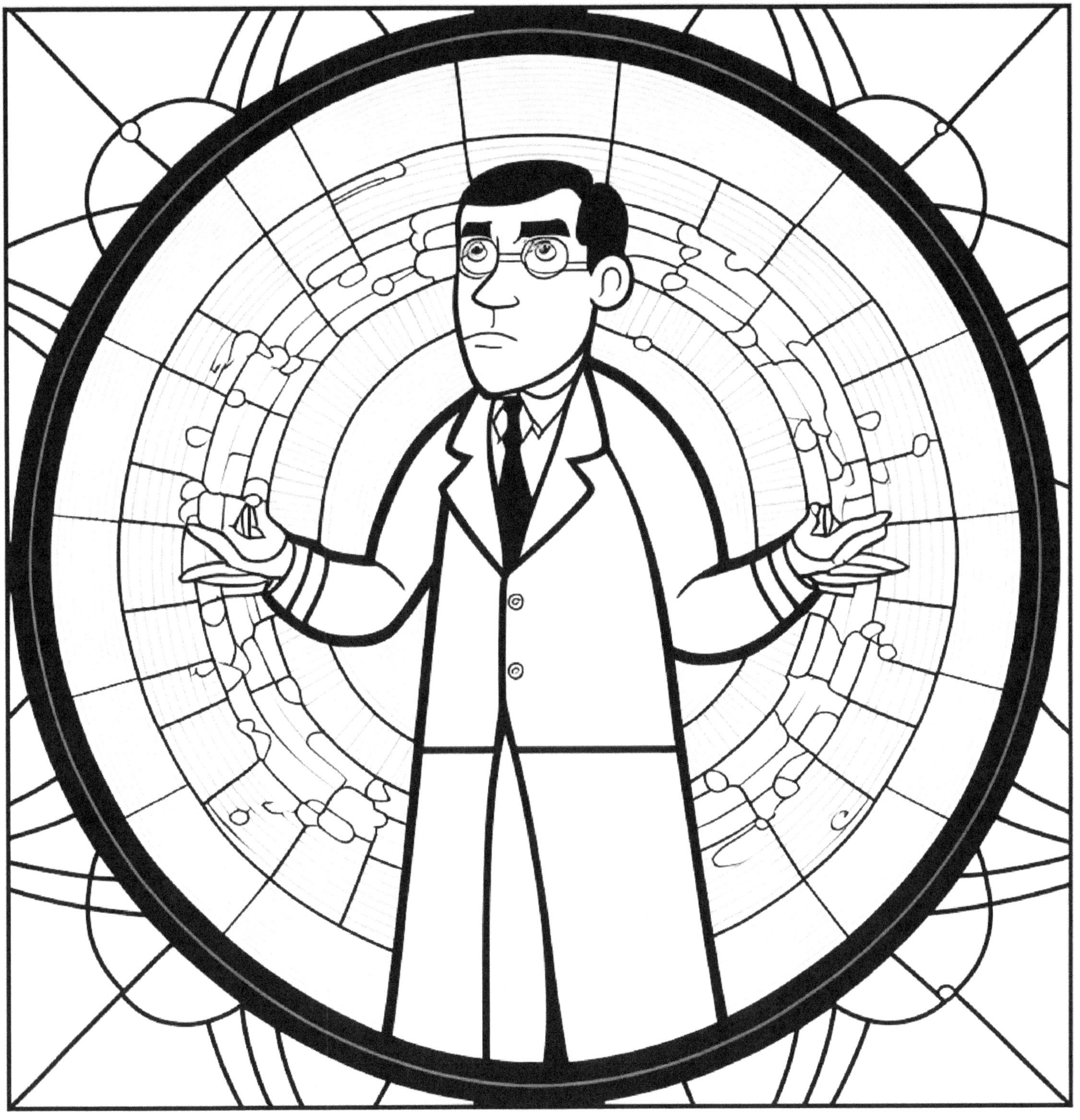

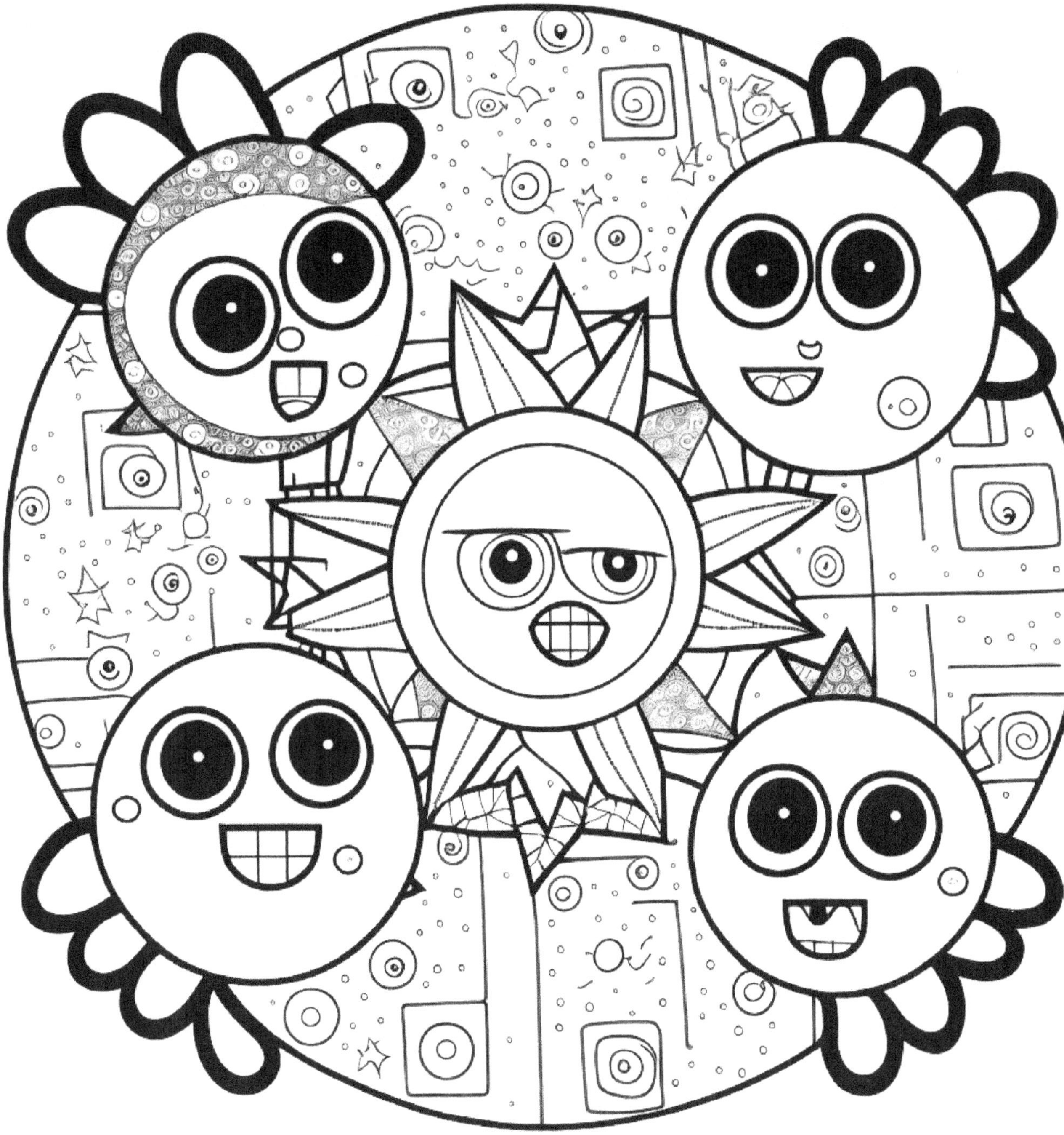

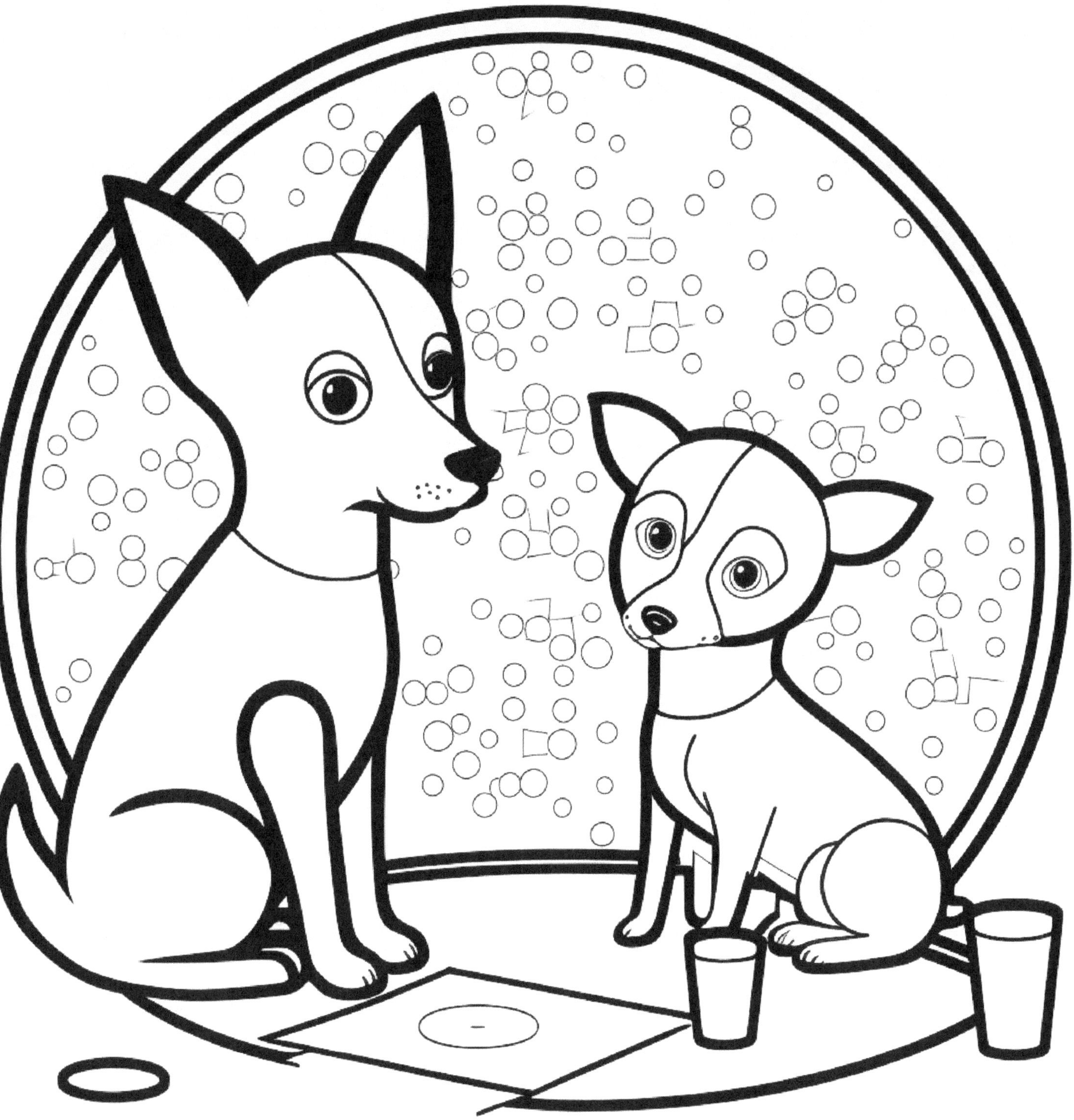

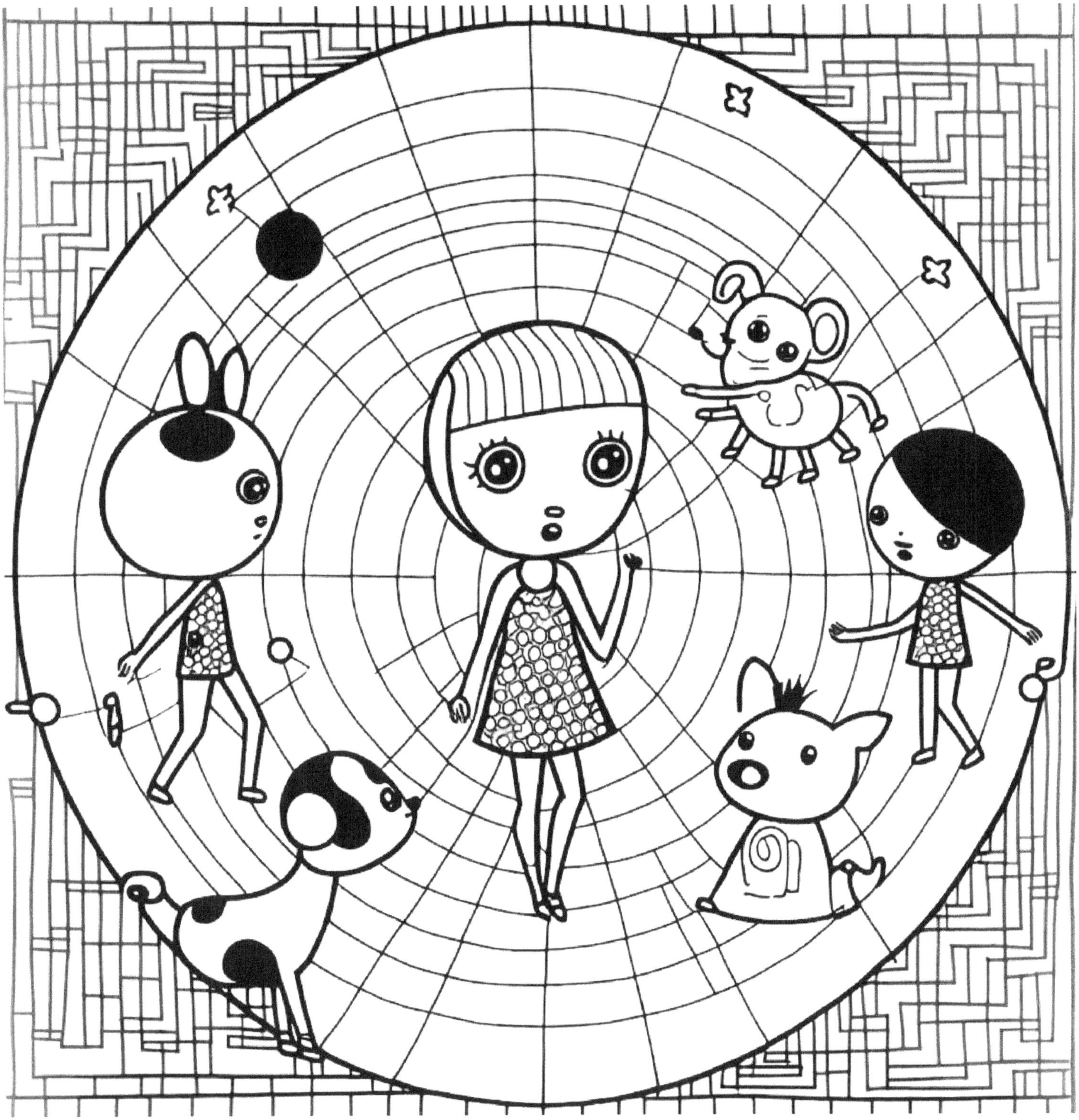

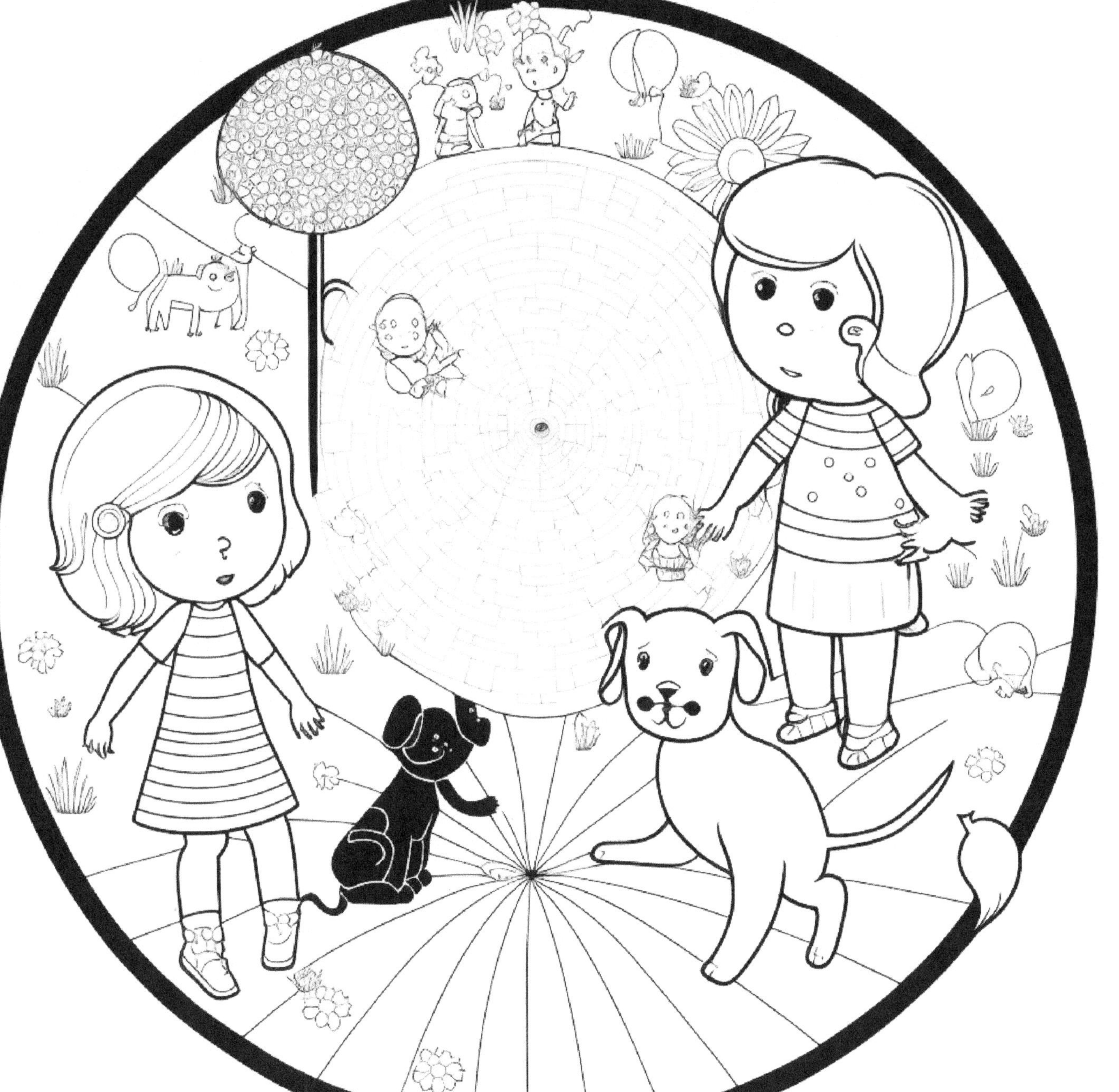

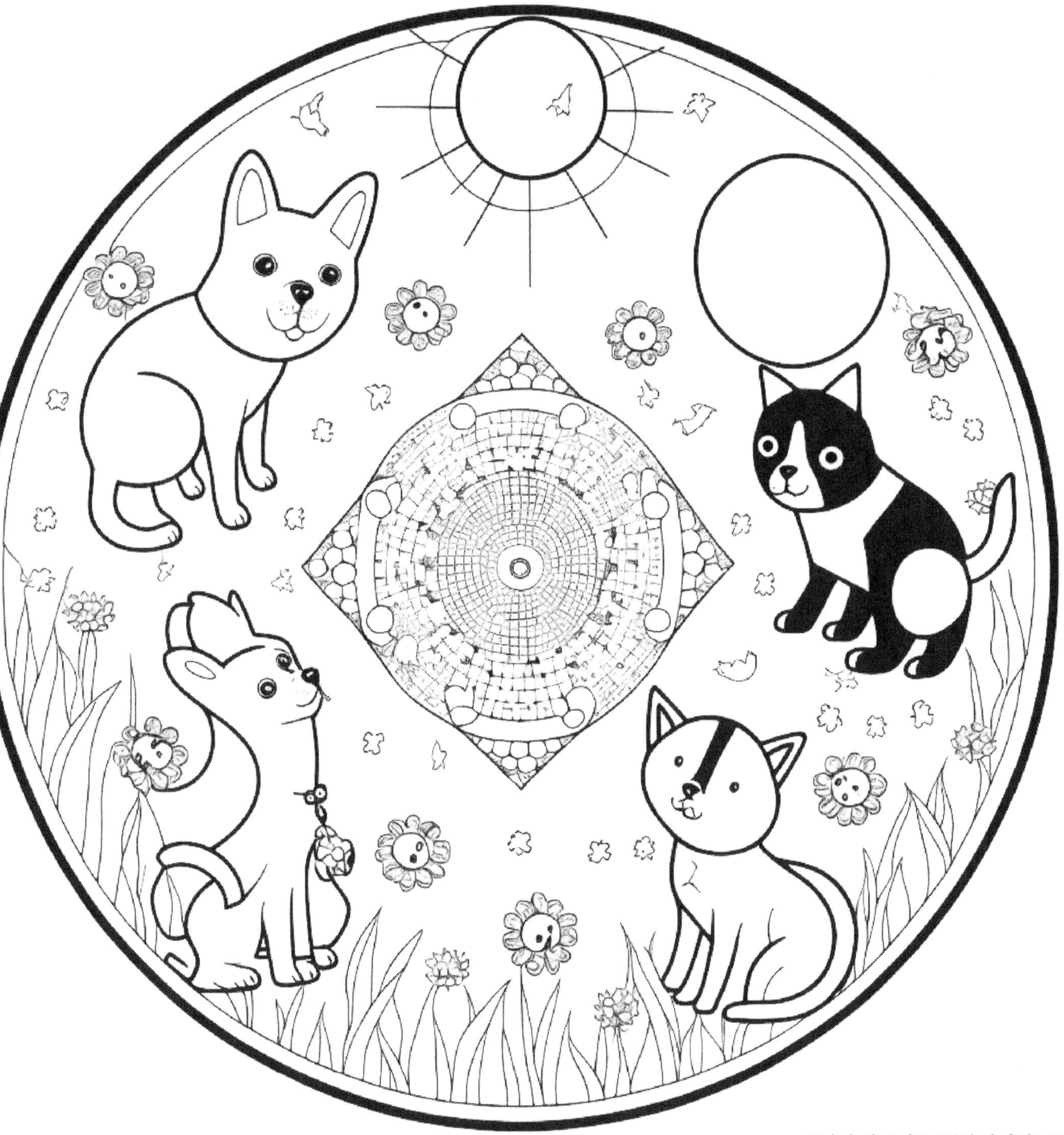

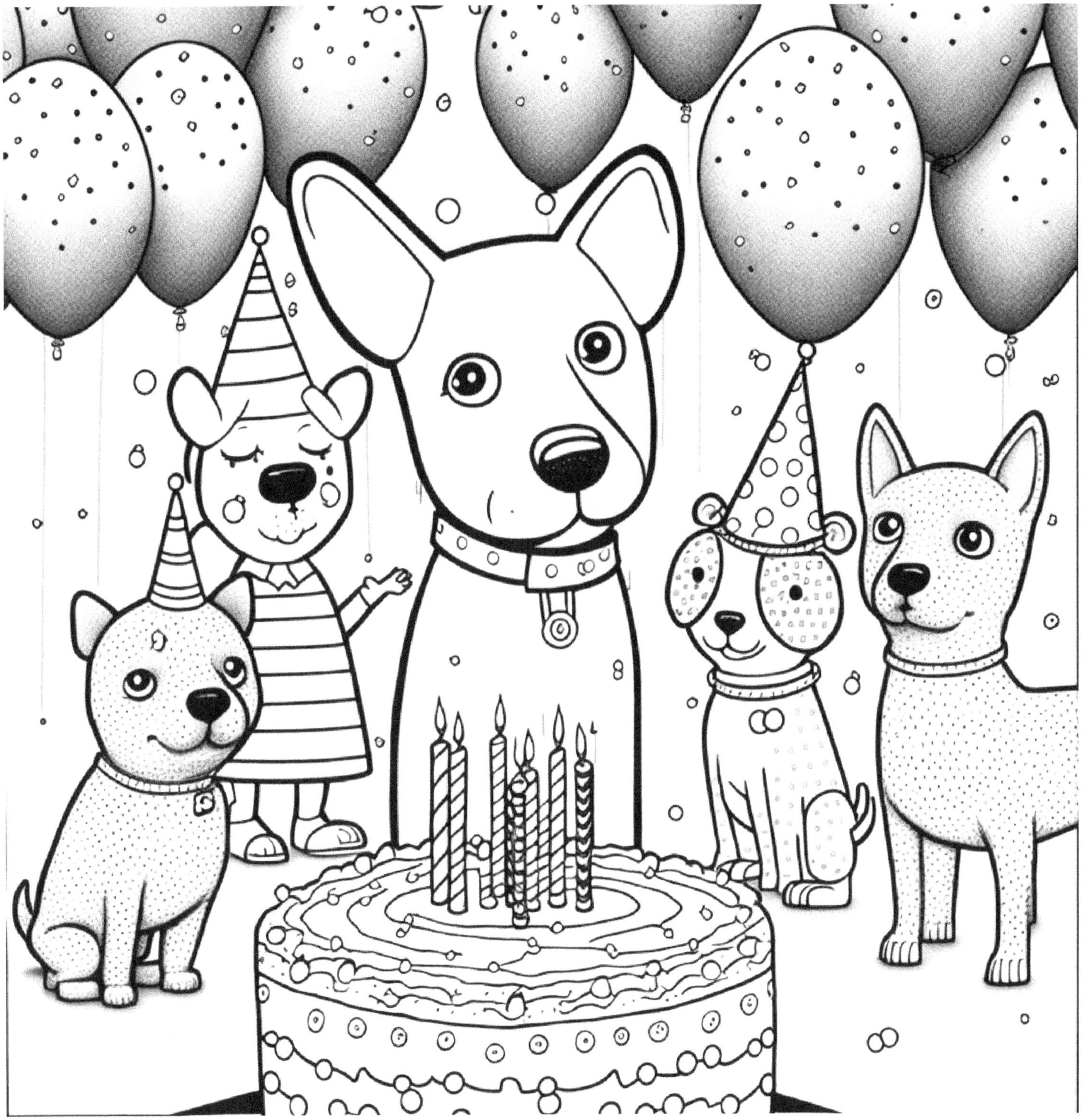

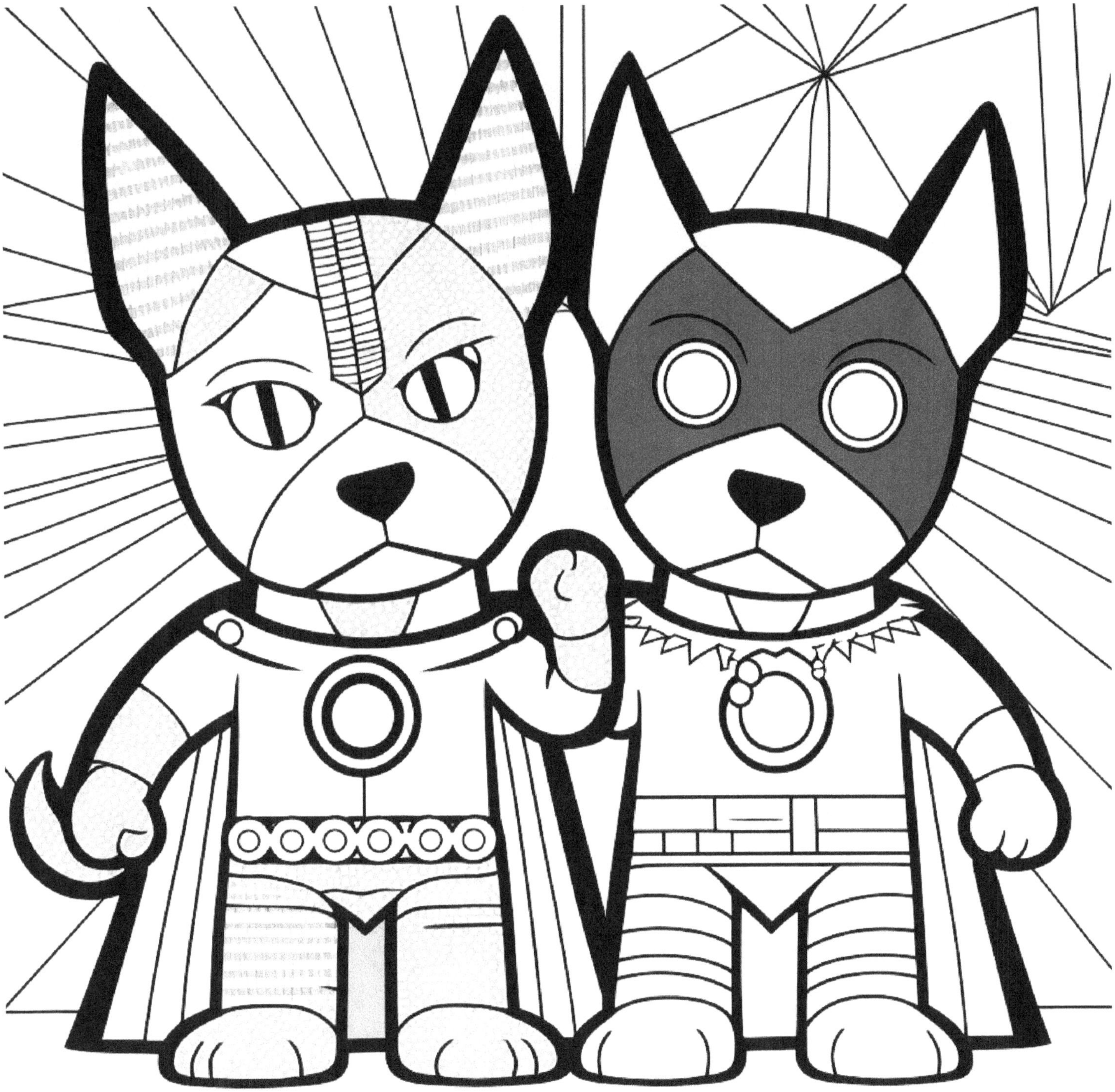

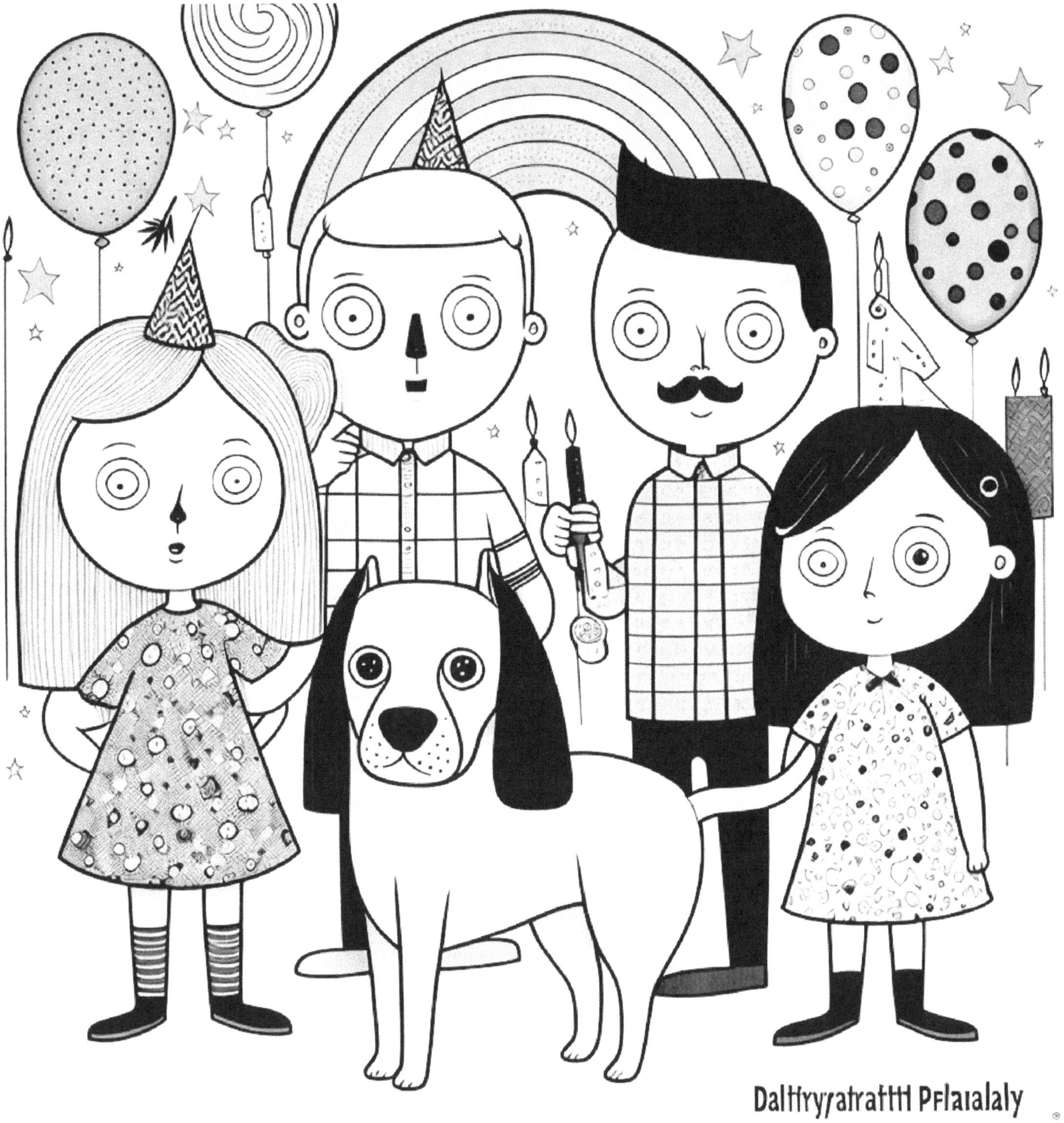

Daltfryyatratttl Pflalalaly

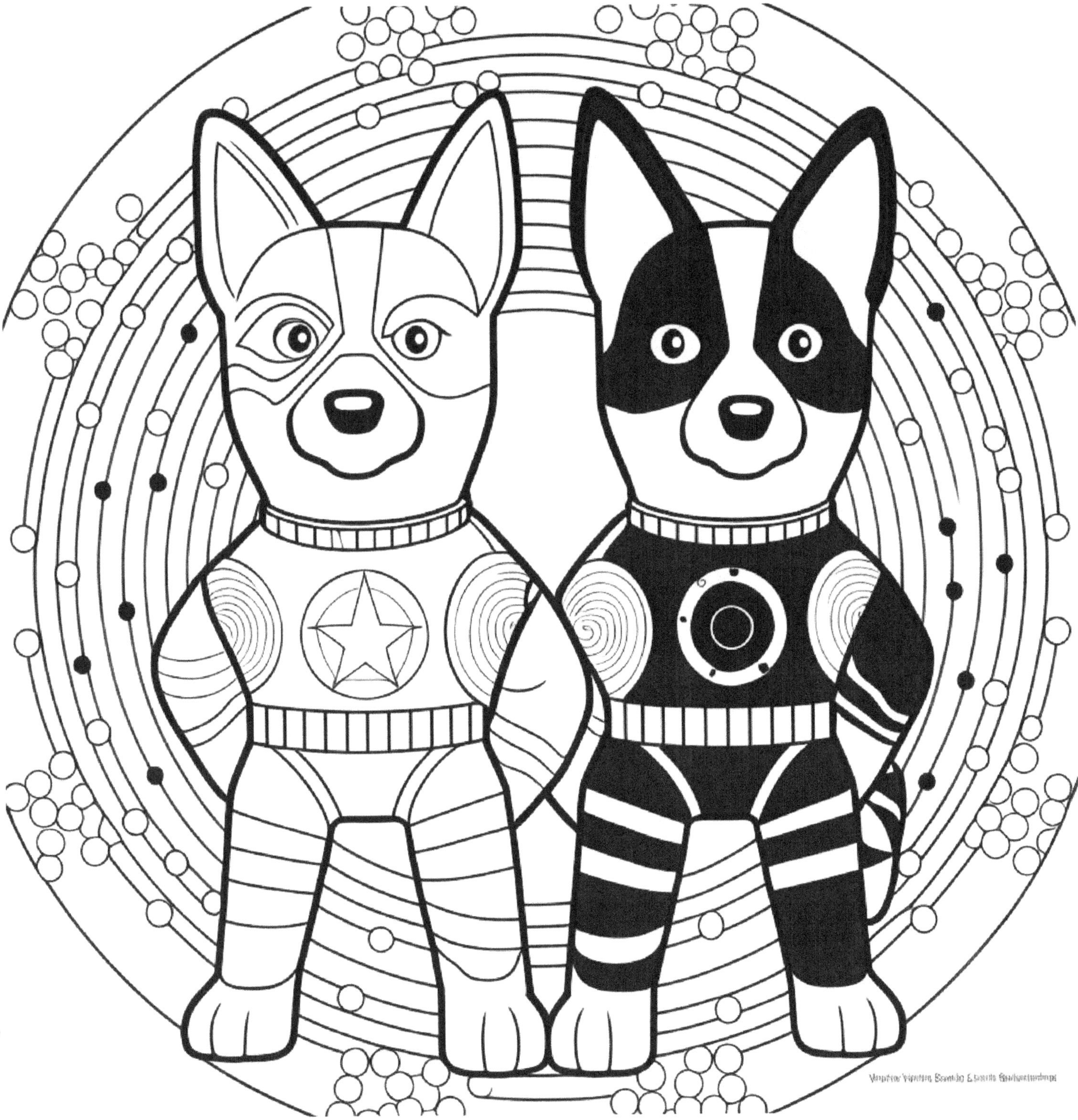

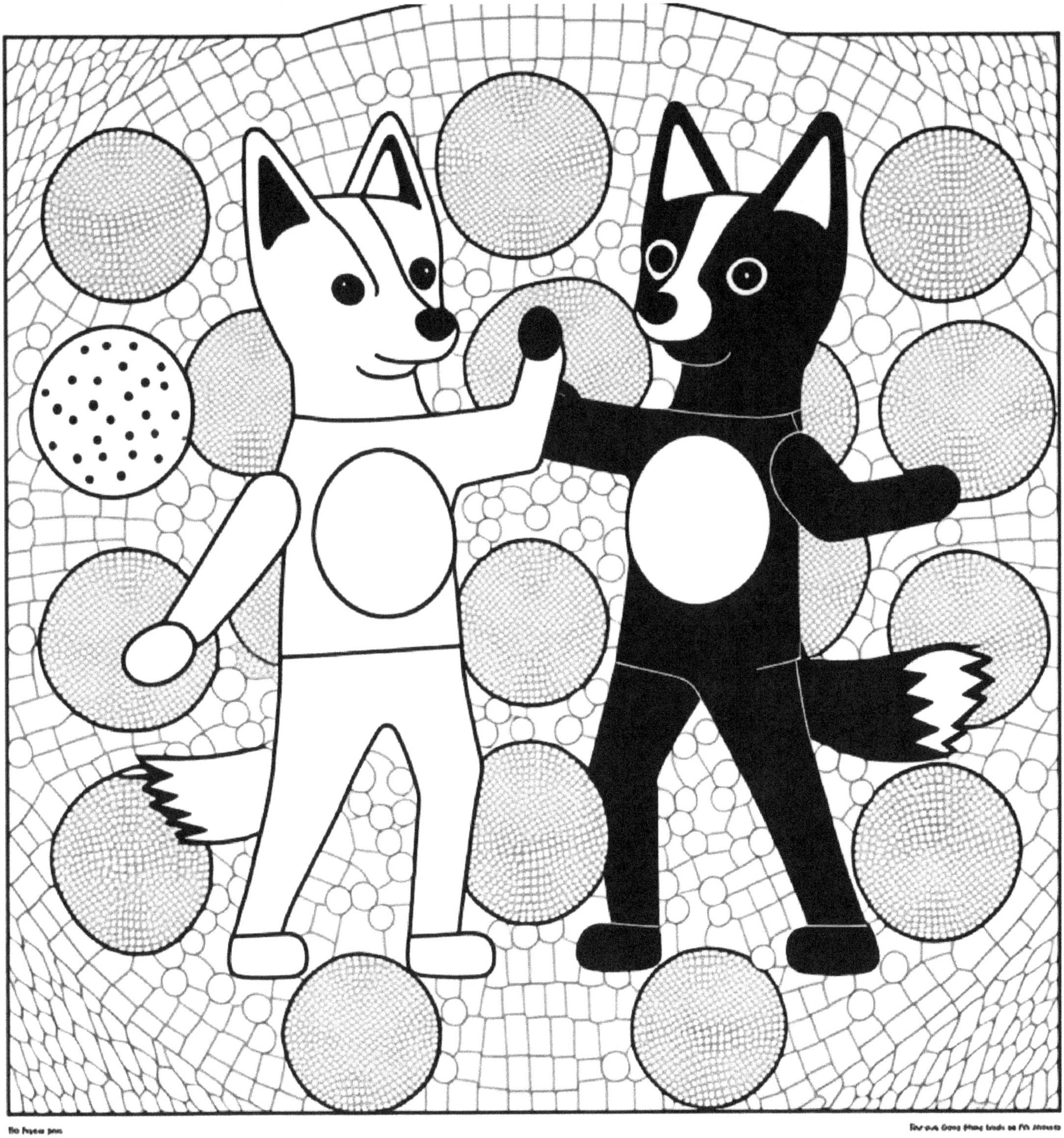

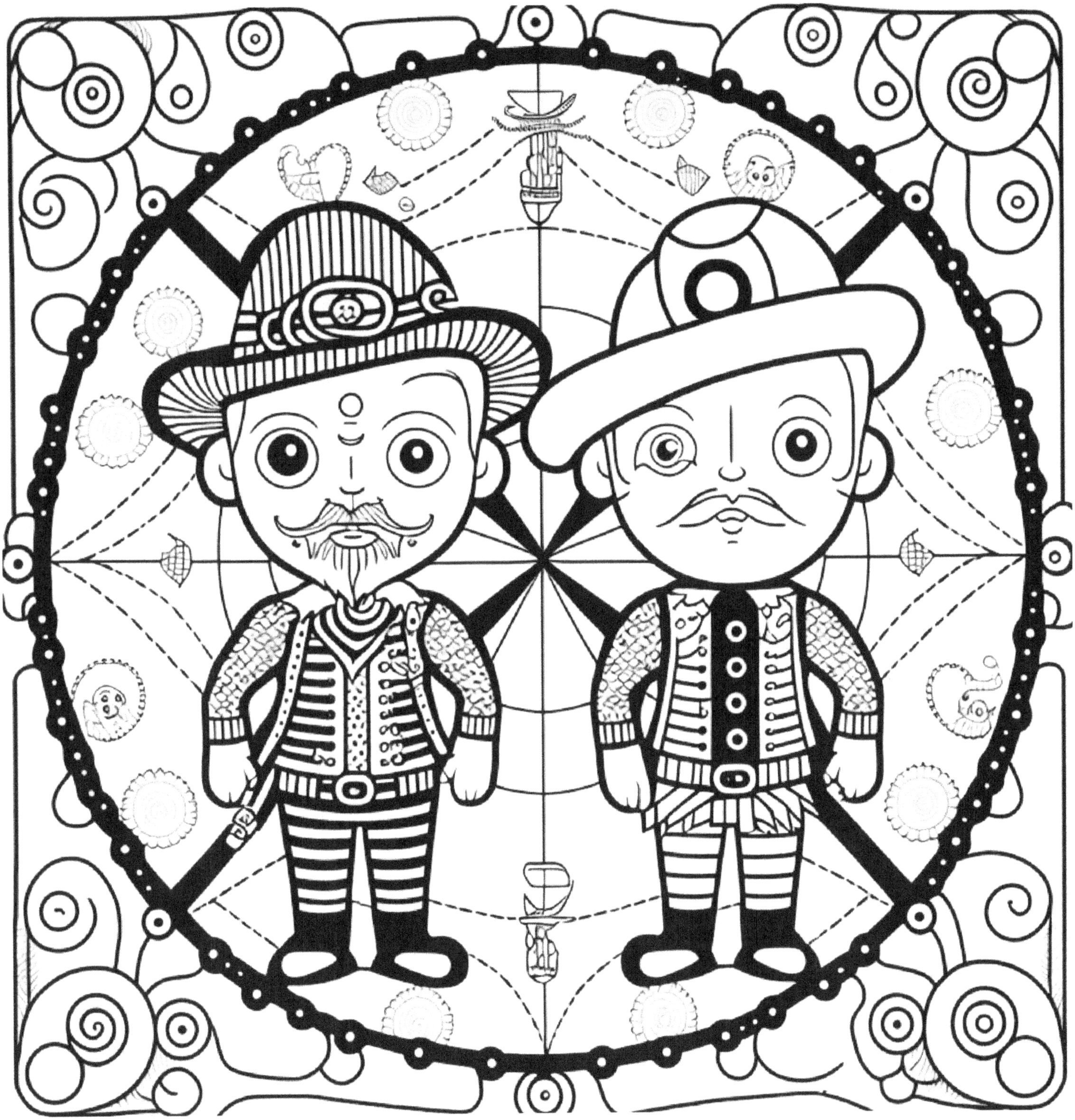

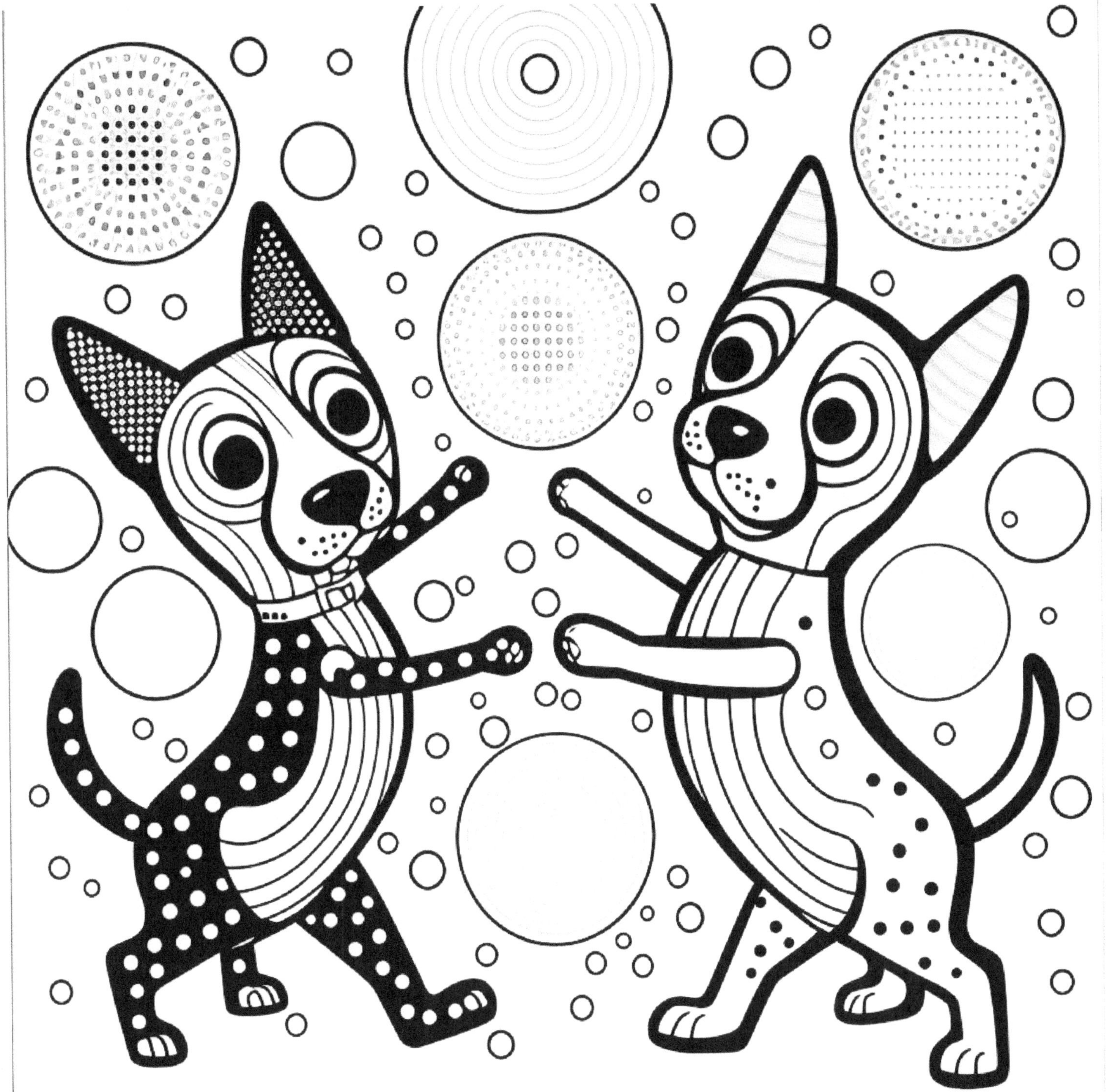

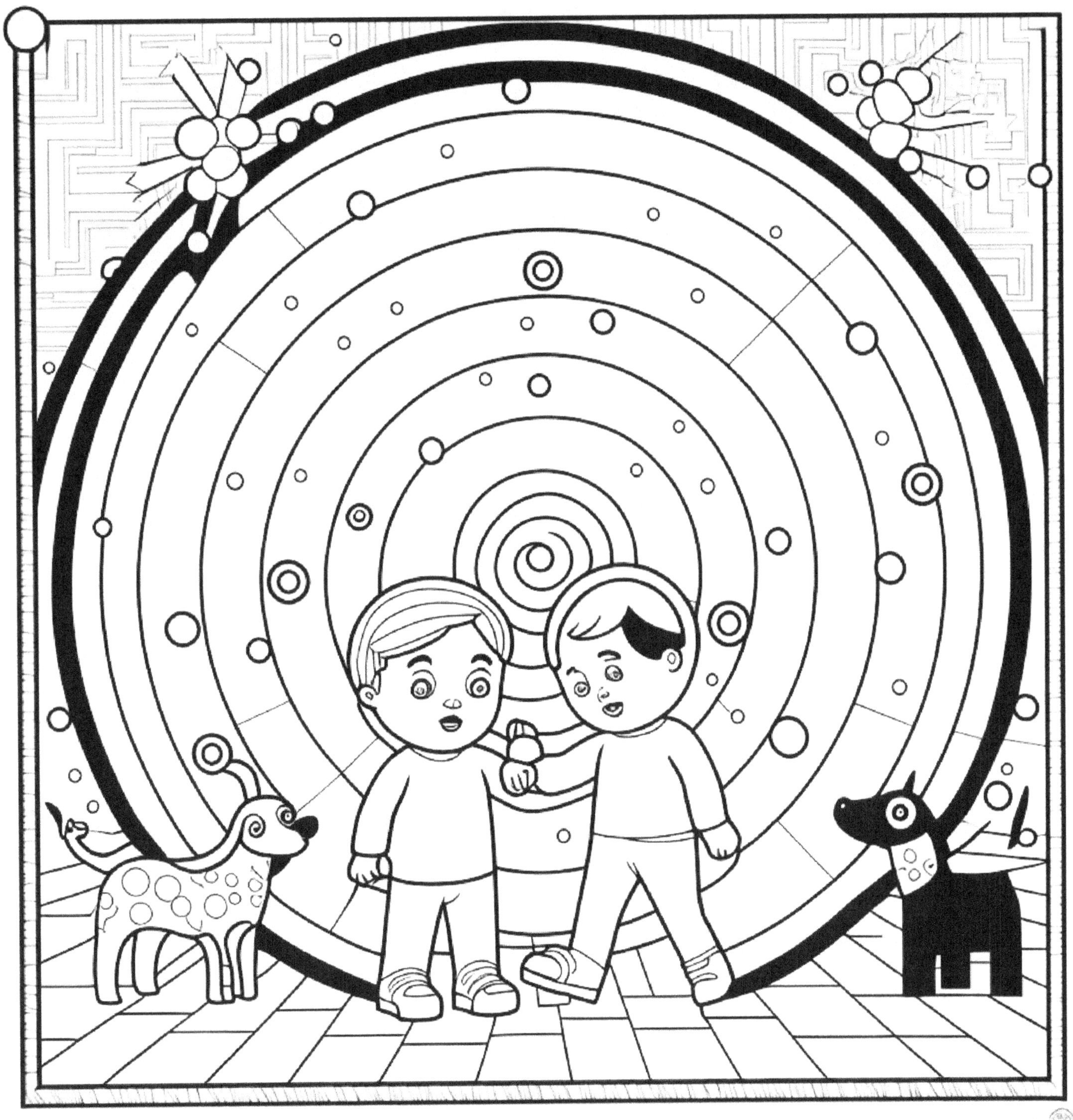

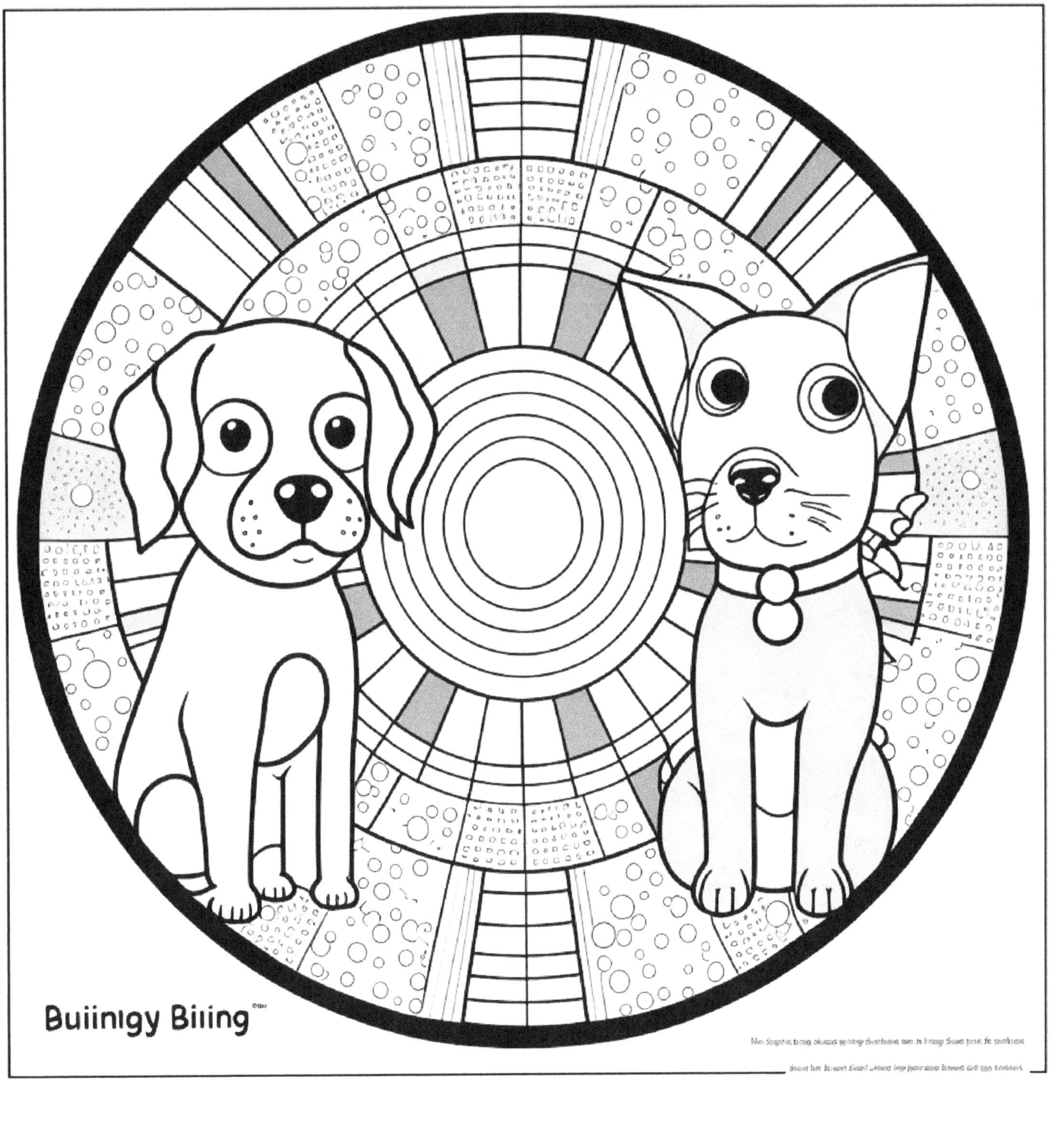

Buiinigy Biiing

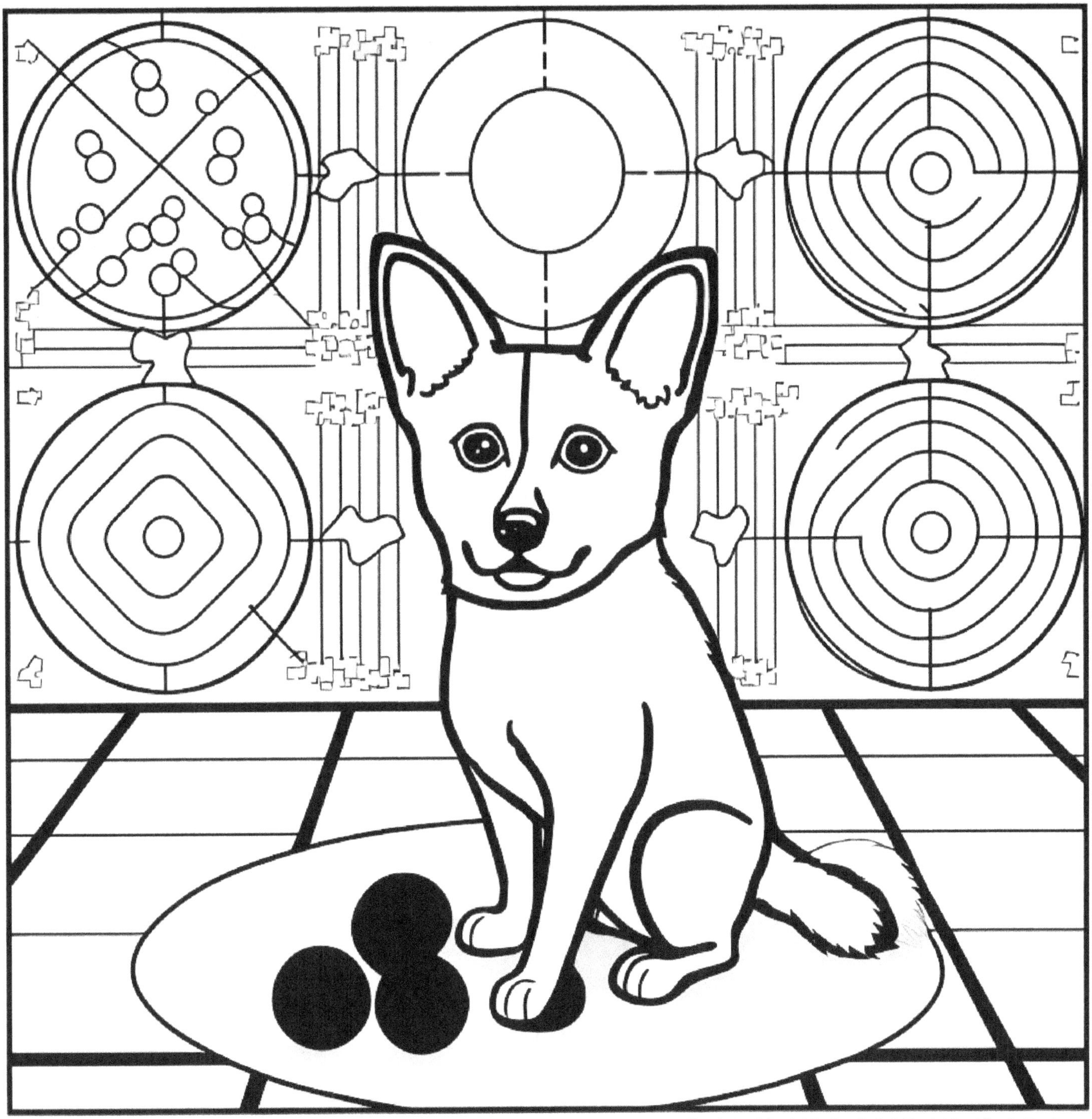

D anylol eol Bayrtdel Chotlbs Doiyalt Roytlal Garel Dosale Bunclicks

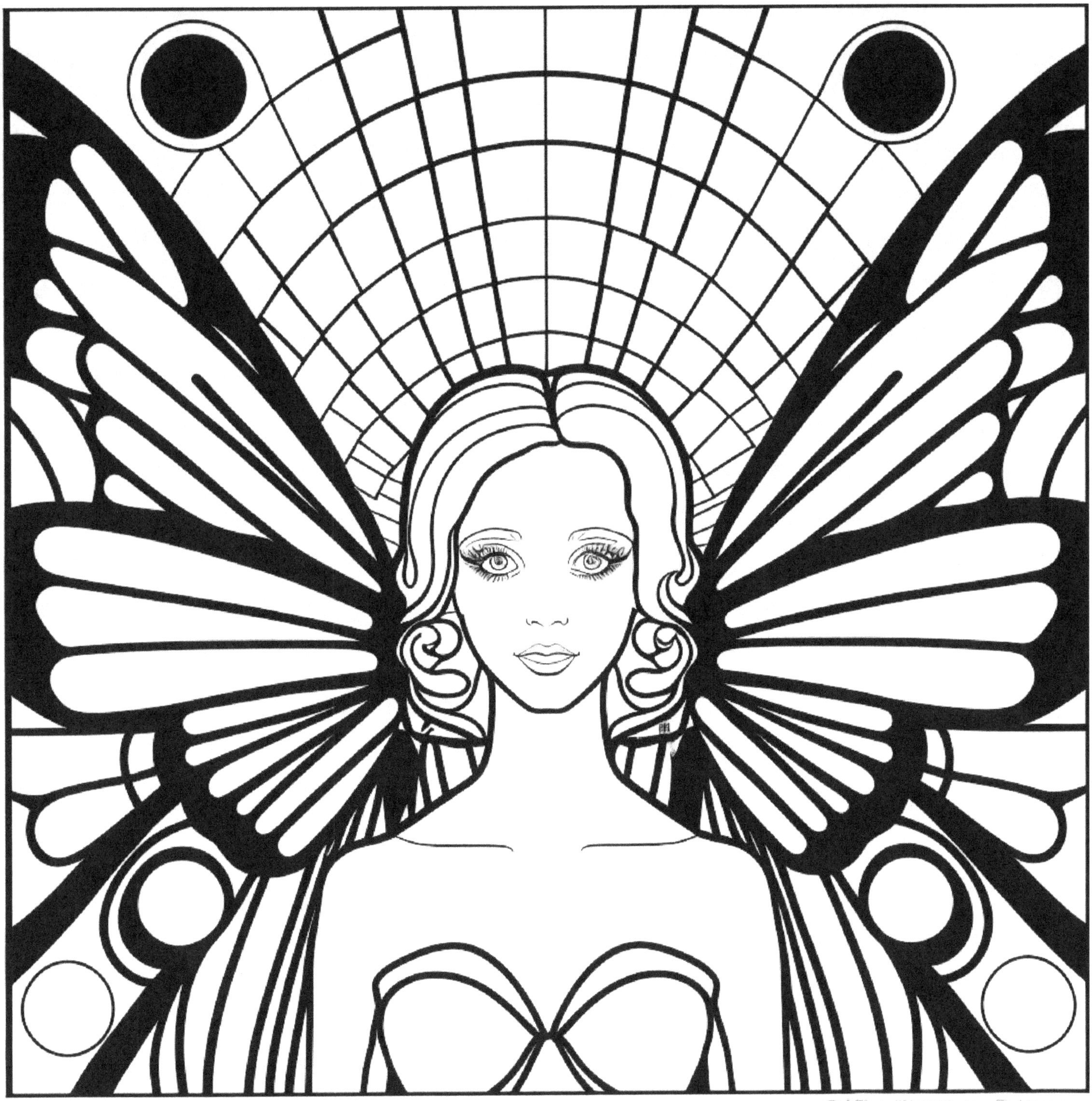

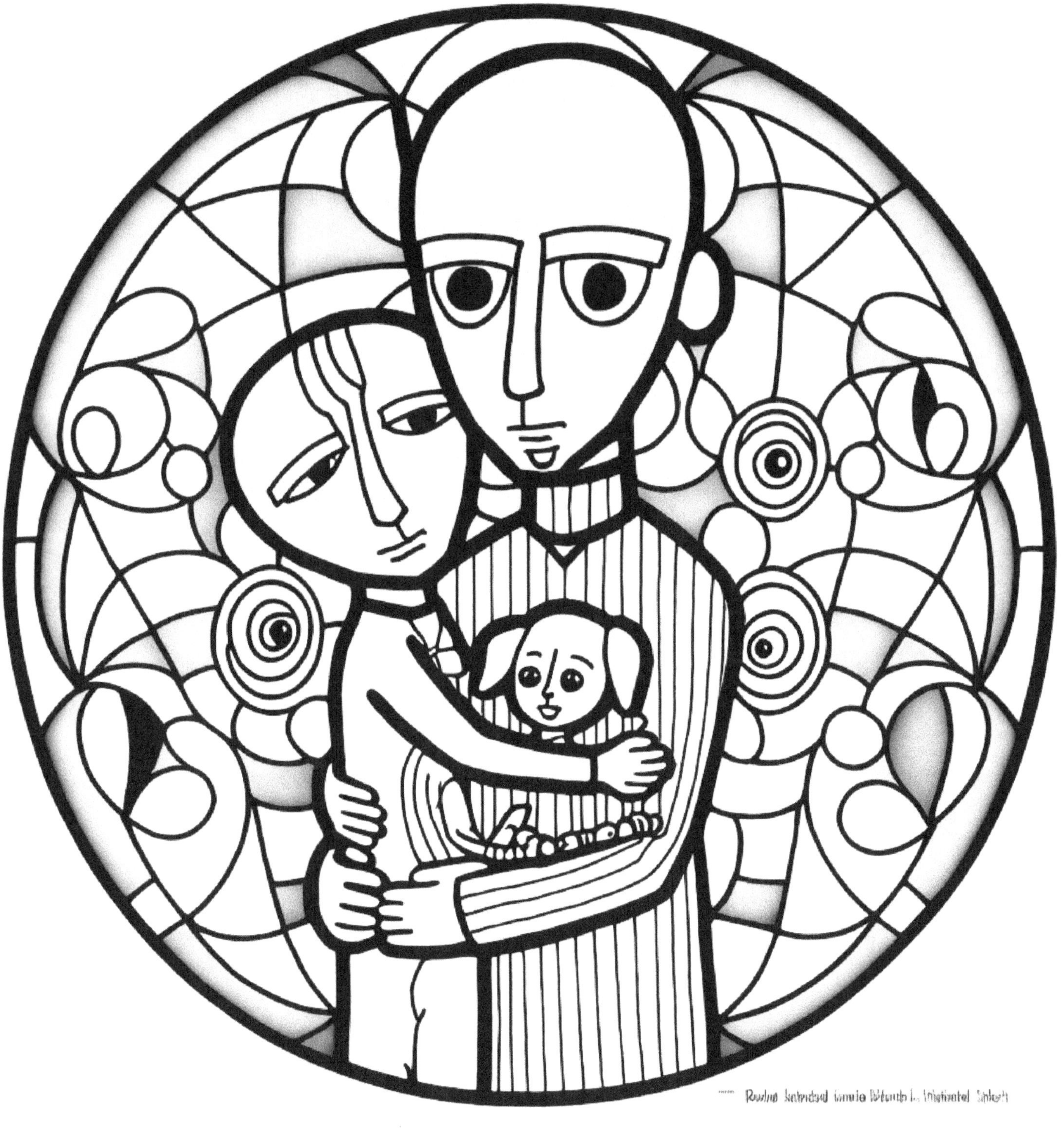

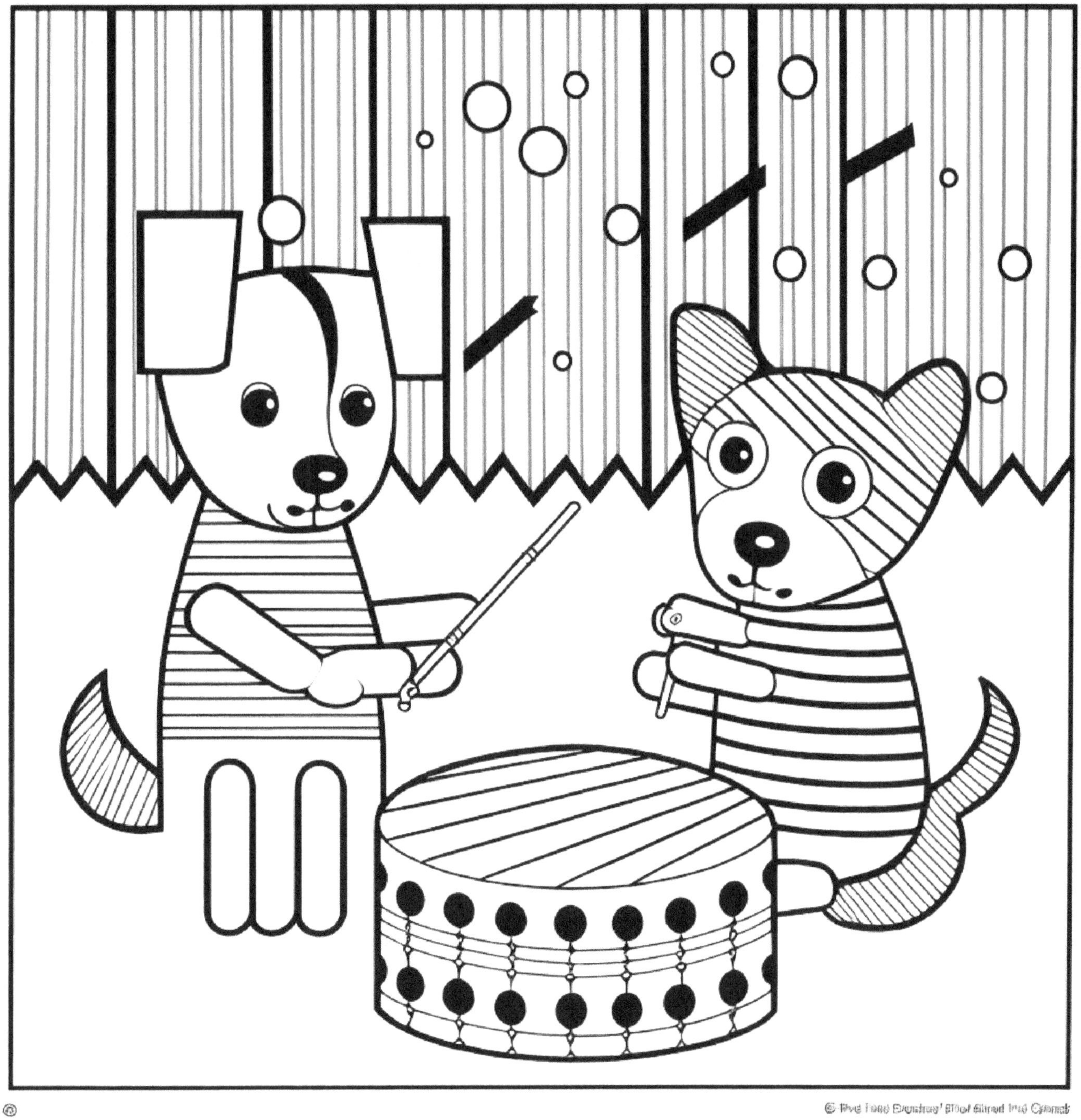

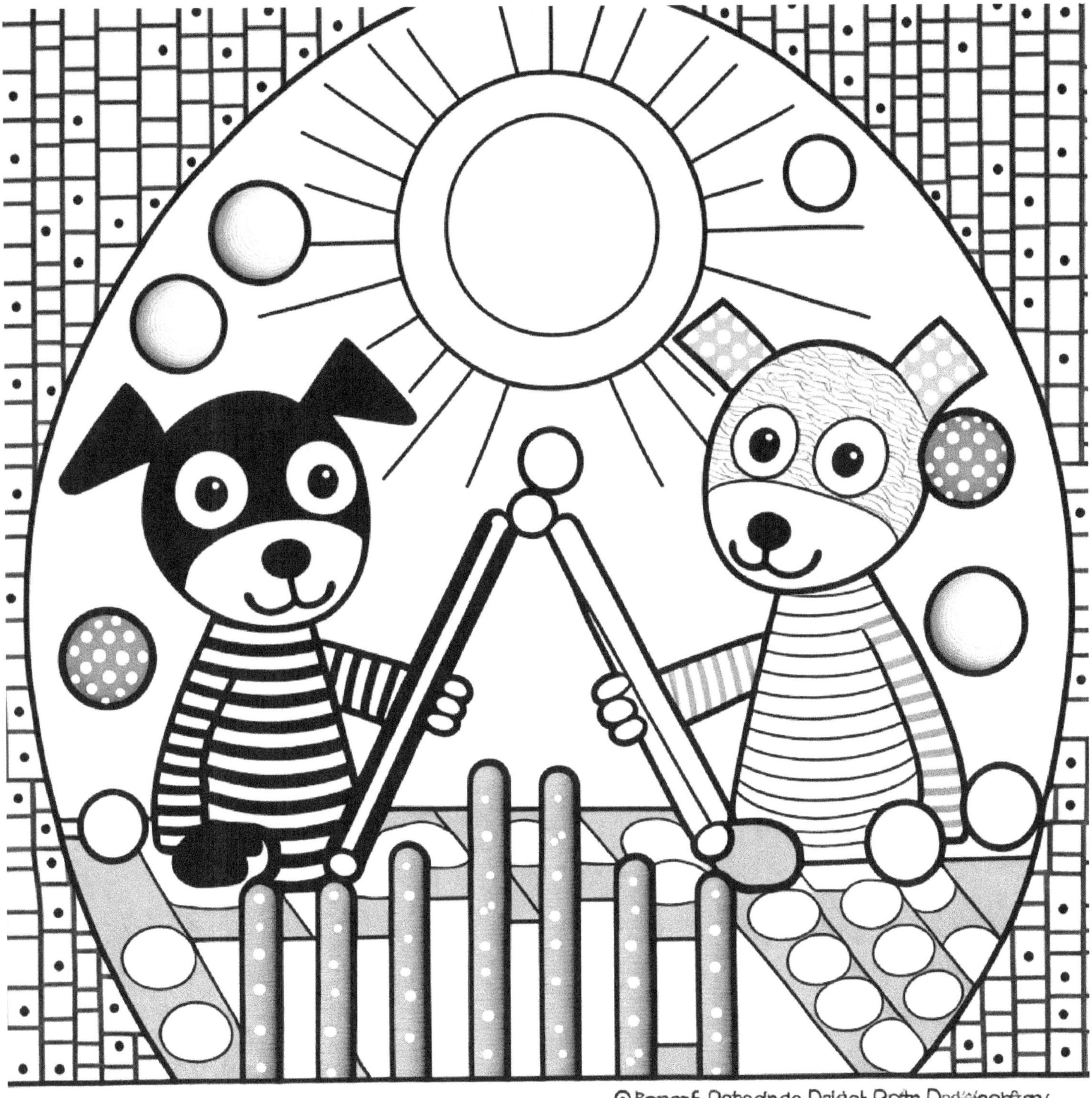

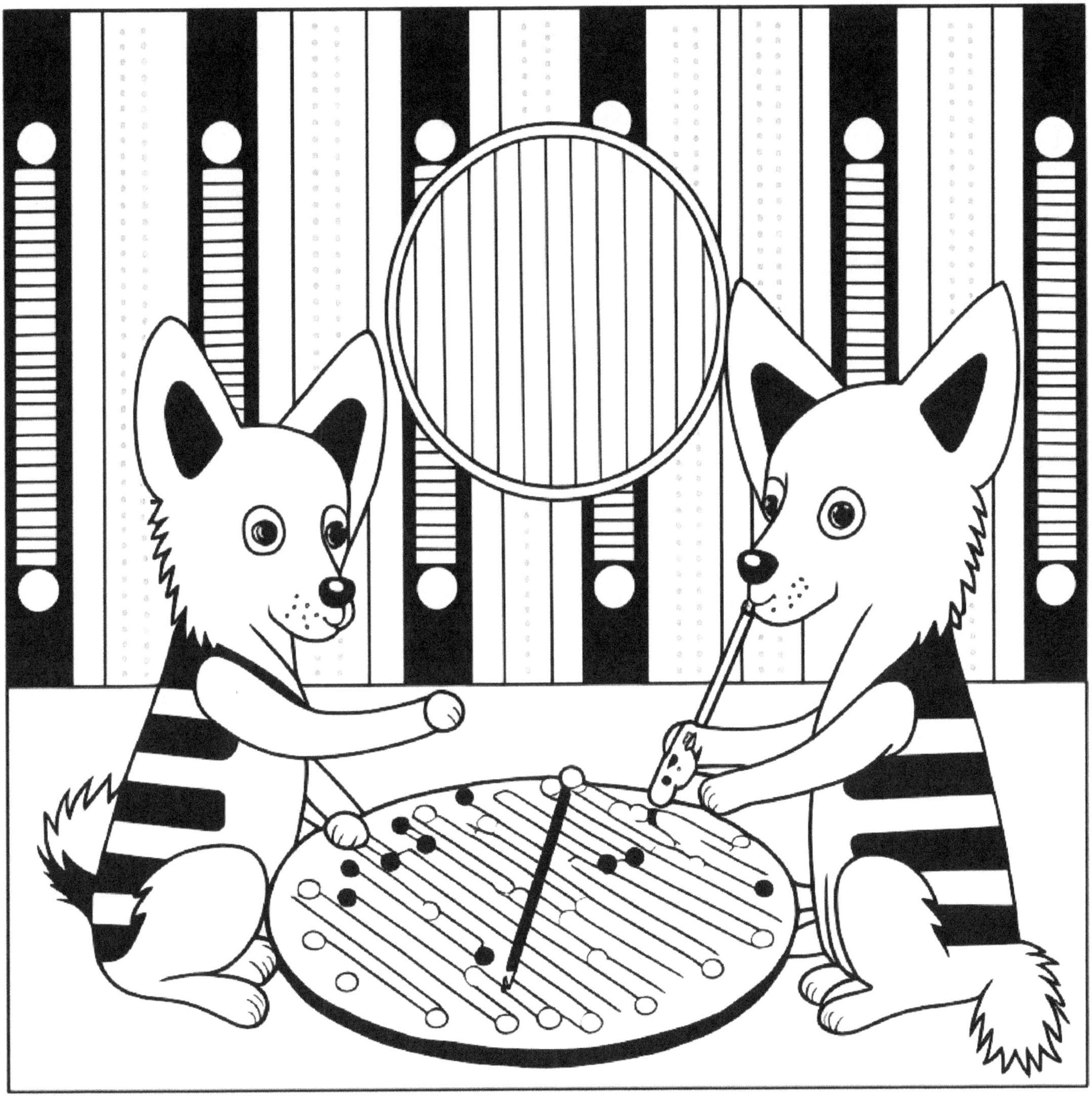

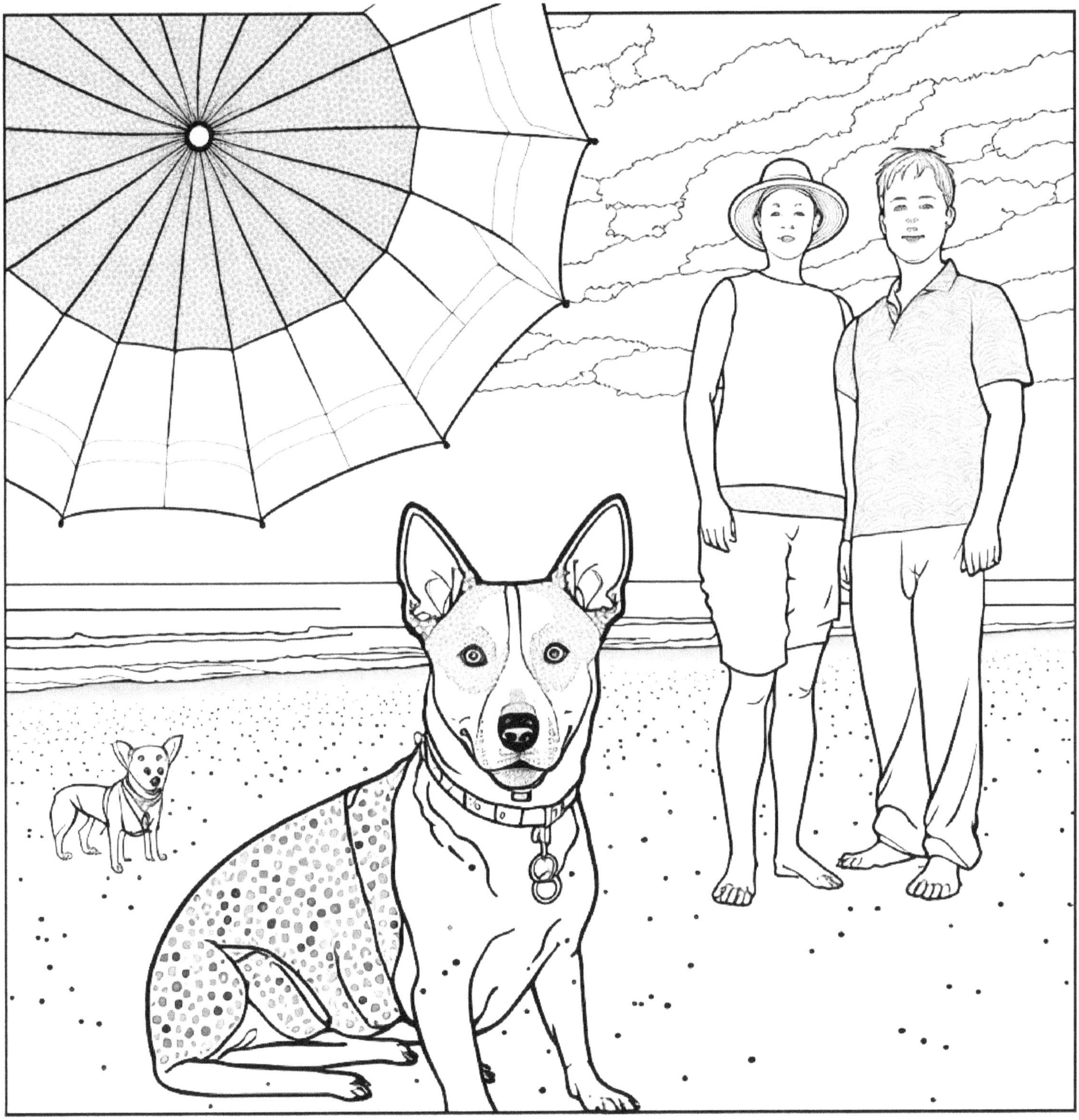

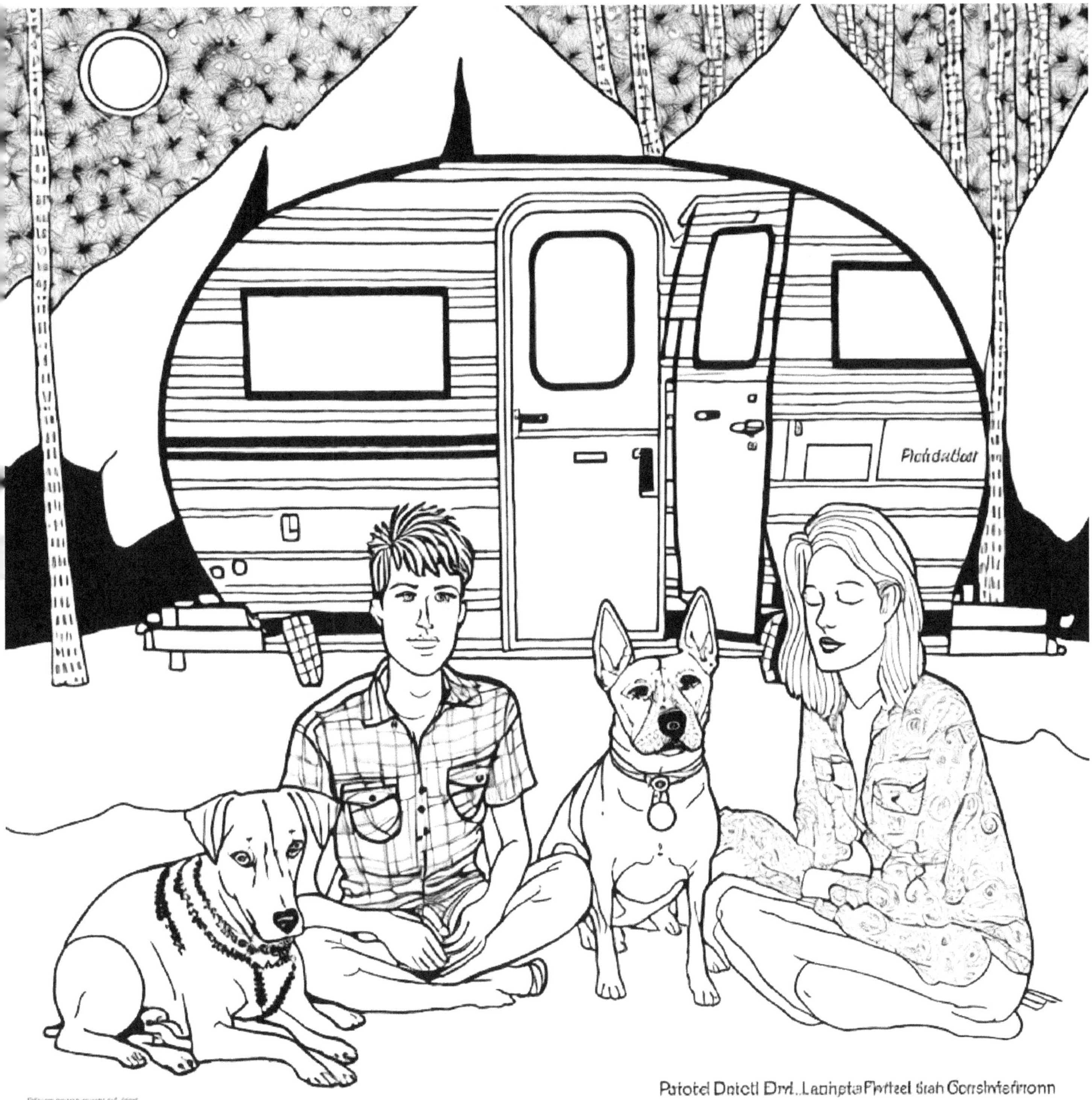

Patotel Dnictl Drd..Lanhpta Fhrtel sah Gorsiwiefronn

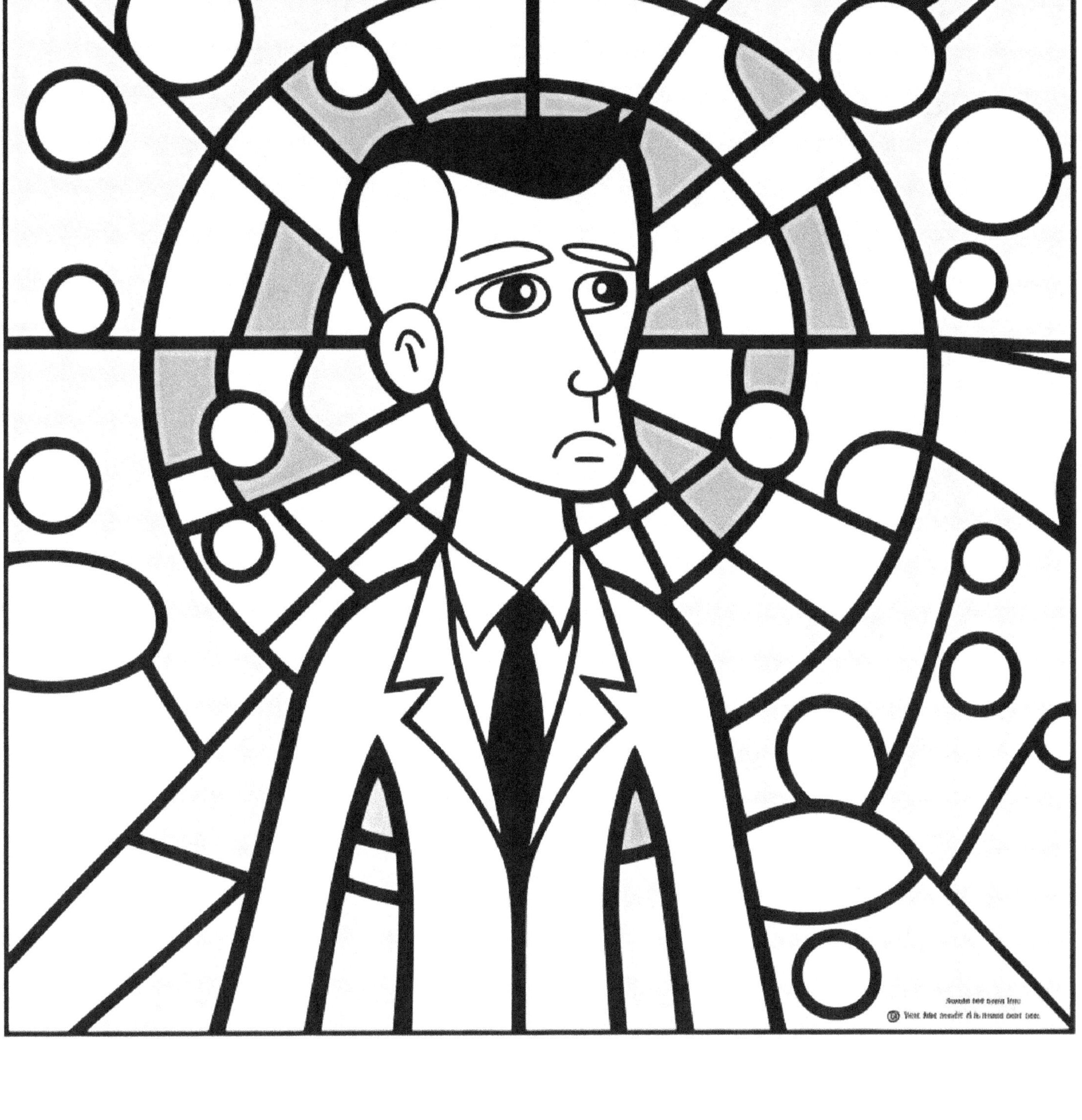

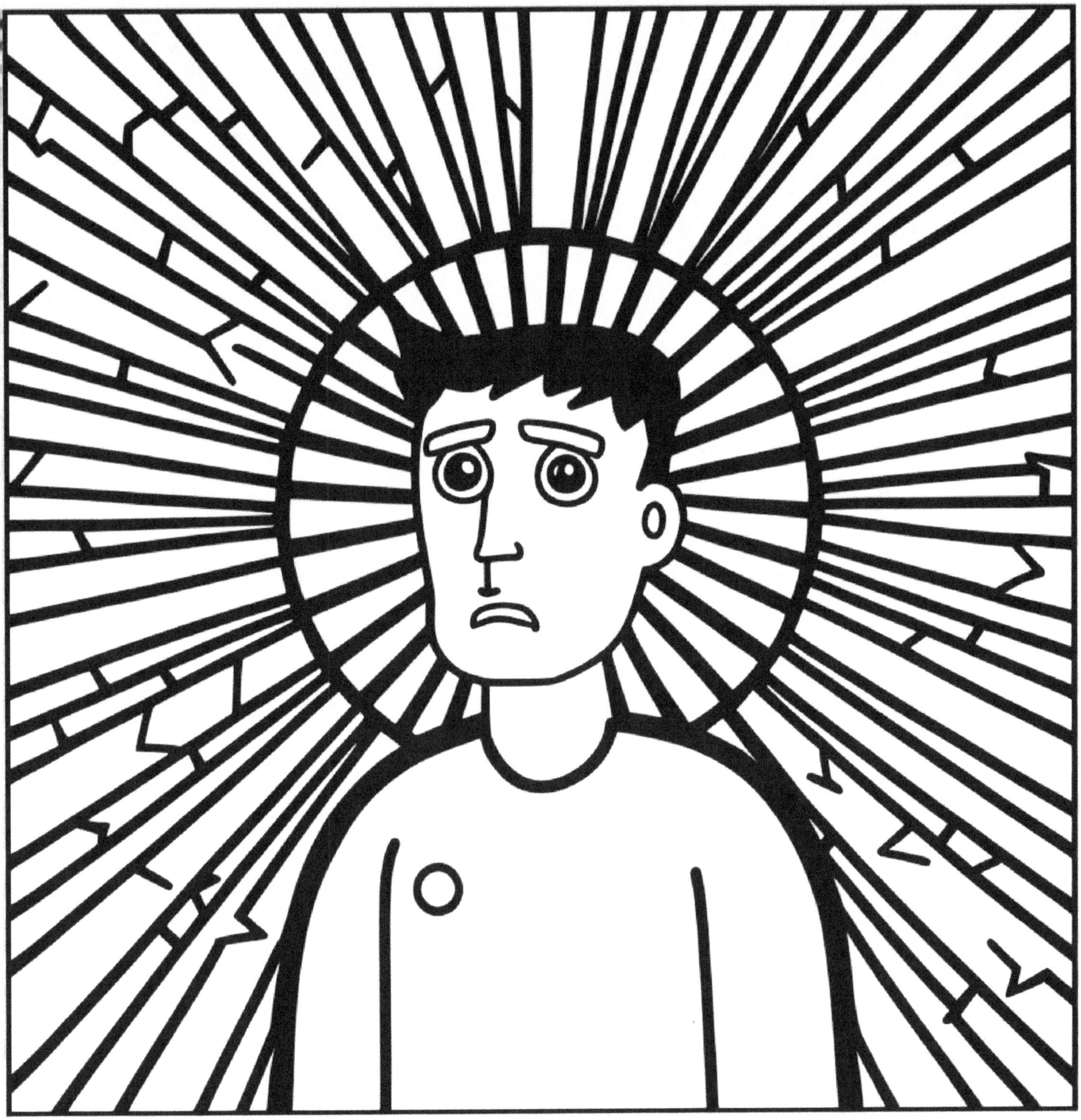

www.ingramcontent.com/pod-product-compliance
Lightning Source LLC
Chambersburg PA
CBHW080107010626
45794CB00015B/3303
9798867948597